1001 WAYS TO PROCRASTINATE

Things to do when you're not doing the things you really should do

Written and illustrated by:

Anthony Rubino, Jr.

CCC PUBLICATIONS • LOS ANGELES

Published by

CCC Publications
21630 Lassen St.
Chatsworth, CA 91311

Manufactured in the United States of America

Cover © 1994 CCC Publications

Interior illustrations © 1994 CCC Publications

Cover & interior art by Anthony Rubino, Jr.

Interior design by Anthony Rubino, Jr.

Interior layout & production by Oasis Graphics

ISBN: 0-918259-58-4

If your local U.S. bookstore is out of stock, copies of this book may be obtained by mailing check or money order for $4.95 per book (plus $2.50 for postage and handling) to: CCC Publications; 21630 Lassen St., Chatsworth, CA 91311.

For information on licensing other works, cartoons & designs by Tony Rubino write to: Creatif Licensing; 31 Old Town Crossing, Mount Kisco, N.Y. 10549.

To my parents, who took great pains to
instill in me a solid, healthy work ethic,
so I could grow up and write a book
devoted exclusively to goofing off.
They must be so proud.

And to my wife Colleen,
the Empress of Procrastination.

When I first came up with the concept for this book, I thought: "Wow! A procrastinator book. Now that's a good idea. I have to put together a proposal for that right away." Two years later I was ready to write one. So I sat down at my computer and feverishly began to play Space Invaders. After that I got myself a soda and took a nap.

A month or so later, I was back at my terminal once again, determined to begin the proposal. Staring intently at the screen, I cracked my knuckles, poised my fingers above the keyboard and noticed that it was really a very nice day outside. So, I went for a walk.

A couple months later I found myself in front of my P.C. once again. I had just typed the words "1001 Ways to Procrastinate" when the phone rang. It was a wrong number. I turned to go right back to work and accidently watched a Brady Bunch marathon on cable for the next nine hours. Whoops.

This sort of thing went on for quite some time until, eventually, I finished the proposal and sold the book. Then all that was left to do was to write and illustrate it. *Piece-a-cake!*

I sat down at my drawing table and... OK. I sat down on the couch and... OK. I lay down on the couch and thought to myself: "I'll have that book written and illustrated in two months. Tops!" A mere 23 months later I was finished.

So in the true spirit of procrastination, wait a few minutes, then turn the page and embark on your journey to a land where nothing ever gets done—a land where time stands still and people stand even stiller—a land where the motto is "Just *DON'T* do it"—where there is no word for responsibility, and where the people have a saying: "Never put off until tomorrow what you can... *ah, never mind. I'll tell ya later.*"

Hesitatingly yours,

Tony Rubino
Tony

"One of these days is none of these days."
—*English Proverb*—

**"Procrastination is the art of
keeping up with yesterday."**
—*Don Marquis*—

**"We are always getting ready to live
but never living."**
—*Emerson*—

"By-and-by is easily said."
—*Shakespeare*—

**"In the sweet old country where I come from,
nobody ever works—nothin' ever gets done."**
—*The Rolling Stones*—

**"Between saying and doing many a
pair of shoes is worn out."**
—*Italian Proverb*—

**"Using famous quotes is an easy way to
take up a whole page in a book."**
—*The Author*—

The List

Before we begin our little journey to Goof-Off Junction, let's take a look at something that can easily become a procrastinator's best friend or *worst nightmare*. Used properly it is perhaps one of the most underrated and cleverly disguised means of procrastination: the list of "things to do."

That's right. Contrary to popular belief, compiling a list of things you *intend* to do *DOES NOT* necessarily get them done. However, if you construct your list properly, you can appear to accomplish quite a bit, *without actually doing anything at all*. It's all a matter of *WHAT* you put on your list. Take a look at the example on the following page, and you'll see what I mean.

HOW ABOUT THAT?!

You're done for the day, and it's not even 9:15 a.m.!

Create Mr. Eraser Man

Bite a pencil eraser halfway through for Mr. Eraser Man's mouth. Then, using your pen, add his nose and eyes. *WOW! His mouth really moves!* Hey Mr. Eraser Man, do you think I should get some work done now?

Do The Ceiling Skewer

Throw ordinary sharpened pencils at the ceiling until you get one to stick. *Whoops,* watch out for those asbestos chips!

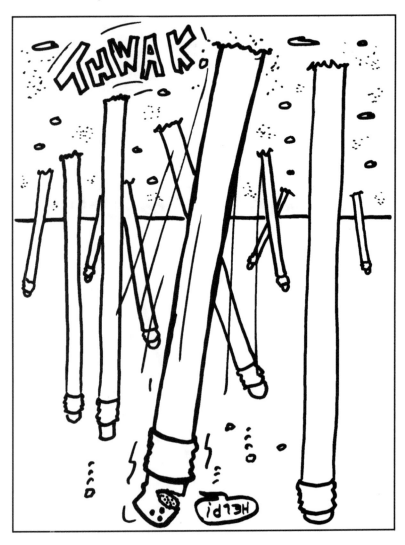

Take Pocket Inventory

Empty your pockets and revel in their contents.

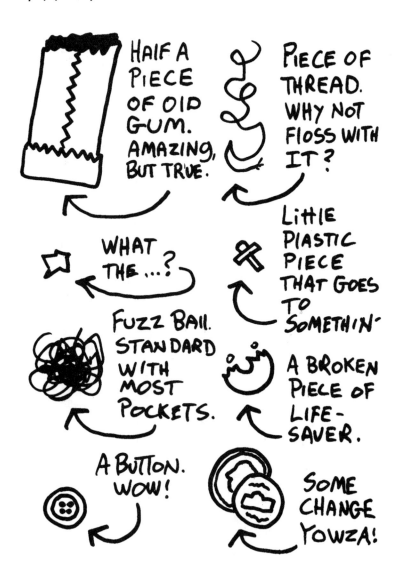

HALF A PIECE OF OLD GUM. AMAZING, BUT TRUE.

PIECE OF THREAD. WHY NOT FLOSS WITH IT?

WHAT THE ...?

LITTLE PLASTIC PIECE THAT GOES TO SOMETHIN'

FUZZ BALL. STANDARD WITH MOST POCKETS.

A BROKEN PIECE OF LIFE-SAVER.

A BUTTON. WOW!

SOME CHANGE YOWZA!

Make a Dandruff Snow Storm

Place your head over a dark surface and scratch it vigorously with both hands to create this incredible simulation of an *icy winter wonderland!*

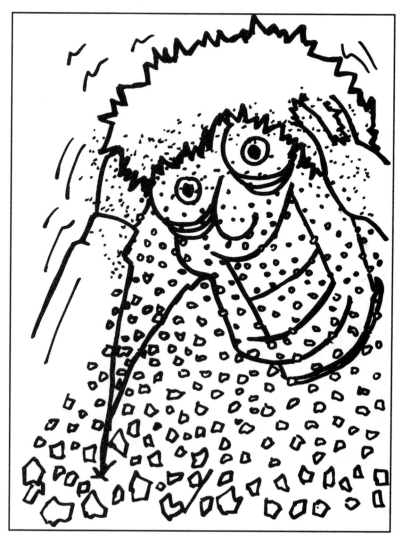

The Super Colossal Never-Ending Star of Eternal Bliss

Step 1: Draw a four point star in the center of a page.
Step 2: Add 3-D lines.
Step 3: Shade thusly.
Step 4: Add points between points.
Step 5: Repeat step #4.

IT NEVER ENDS!

Make a
Rubber Band Ball

Tie three or four rubber bands into a tight knot. Then start tightly wrapping more rubber bands around the knot. The spherical shape will begin to take form all by itself. Before you know it…*BOING! It's a ball!* Watch it grow into a golf ball, a softball, a basketball, *A BEACH BALL!!*

Play With Your Rubber Band Ball

Don't let all that hard work go to waste. Use that rubber band ball to *goof off some more!*

Create The Illusion of The Rubber Pencil

Step 1: Very lightly grasp a pen or pencil at its mid-point with your thumb and forefinger.

Step 2: Now hold it, horizontally, about a foot in front of you.

Step 3: While staring at the utensil, loosely shake your hand up and down while wiggling the pencil from side to side and... HOLY *HOUDINI! It's magic!*

Gossip

What's that you say? You don't have anything *juicy* to talk about. Don't let that stop you! *Make stuff up!*

Launch Yourself Across The Room

That's right! Sit in a chair with wheels, and plant your feet up against a desk or wall. Then count backward from 10 to 1* and *BLAST OFF!* It's *fun!* It's *thrilling!* And best of all, *it kills time!*

Make believe pre-launch conversation with Houston Control, optional.

Spin Your Way To Happiness

Relive those childhood days when you'd spin around in circles just to see how long it would take you to fall down. Only this time use your swivel chair.*

Spin before lunch for best results. Spin in opposite direction to un-dizzy yourself.

Target Practice

Test your marksmanship by trying to hit small objects with rubber bands.

Doodle*Update*

The Bleed Deed

Rest an ordinary felt tip pen on a notebook page, applying light pressure for 2 minutes to 1 hour. Then try to guess how many pages it bled through. *Do you think you can get it to bleed through the whole pad?! It's bleedarific!*

Make Origami Snow Balls

Take an ordinary piece of paper and sculpt it into a beautiful origami snowball. *Wow!* You can easily see why this beautiful and ancient art form has survived throughout the centuries.

Play Some Hoops

Use those very same origami snowballs, a wastebasket, and a little imagination and before you can say, "Oh dear God in heaven, I'm bored out of my stinkin' skull." *You're going one-on-one with Michael Jordan!*

Straighten out a Paper Clip

Hey! It's just a wire after all! Who'd have thought?

Break Solid Steel With Your Bare Hands

Take a straightened paper clip and start bending it back and forth, back and forth, back and forth, *BUT DON'T LET IT BREAK YET*, because this is a double treat! Just before the clip breaks, feel the metal at its weakest point. *YOUCH! That's right! The friction has caused the metal to get WARM!* O.K., now *break it.*

Make a Little Man

Use your straightened paper clips as arms and legs, and an origami snowball for a torso. Then draw a little face for your new friend. *Well, would you look at this! It's Mr. Origami Clip Man! Hey Mr. Origami Clip Man, do you think I oughta get some work done now?!*

Untangle Your Phone Cord

Measure Your Body Parts

Ever wonder *exactly* how long a body part is? Well stop wonderin' and start measurin'!

Doodle*Update*

Holes-O-Fun

Use the binder holes in your notebook as facial orifices for hours of *zany cartoon madness!*

Call a Friend or Relative and Talk About Absolutely Nothing

Snap, Crackle And Pop

Crack your finger and toe knuckles. Twist 'em, pull 'em, yank 'em, bend 'em, snap 'em, crack 'em, for hours of joint poppin' fun.

Color-In Your Entire Desk

Situate yourself at a desk in the back of your classroom. now, in stead of listening to your teacher or professor drone on about valuable information essential to your future, grab your pencil and go to work. Using small strokes (so as not to attract attention) start at the top left corner and *simply cover that entire 2" by 2" square of school property with lead!* It ain't easy, but it *CAN* be done!

Bowling for Pennies

Draw a bowling lane on a piece of paper or some other smooth surface. Use pennies for pins, and a nickel for the bowling ball. Flick the nickel down the lane with your index finger and— *STEEEEEEERIKE!*

Take Apart Your Pen

Disassemble your pen, and marvel at the complex simplicity of Mr. Ballpoint's greatest invention.

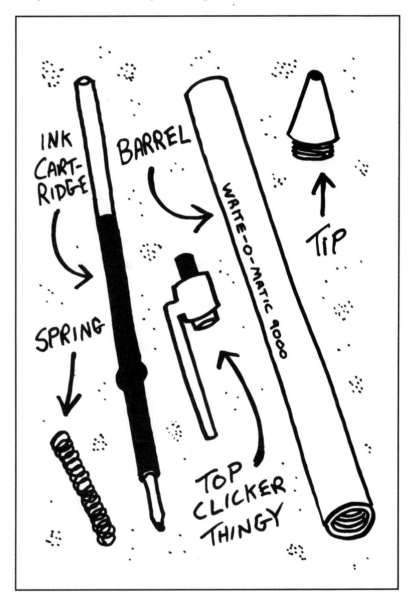

The Spring Thing

Take that little spring inside your pen, grasp it between your thumb and forefinger and *"boing"* it *across the room!*

Doodle*Update*

Galactic Fever

Step 1: Draw a heavily inked dot on your desk or any other smooth surface.

Step 2: Before the ink dries, run your finger across it and—*MY STARS—it's a comet!*

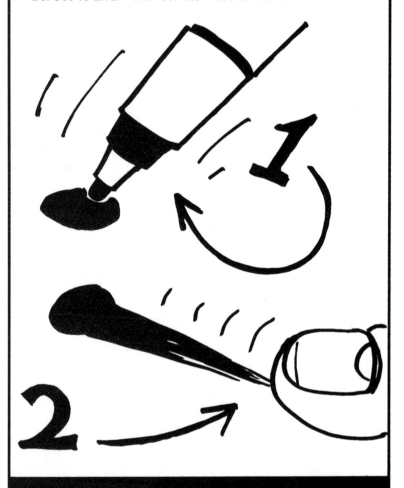

Get Some Coffee— Let it Get Cold— Get Some More

Create Phantom Gum

Unwrap a stick of gum and chew it. Now carefully re-fold the wrapper so it looks like it has gum in it. Not only does it waste time, but when you're done you'll think to yourself, *"WOW, that really looks like it has gum in it!"*

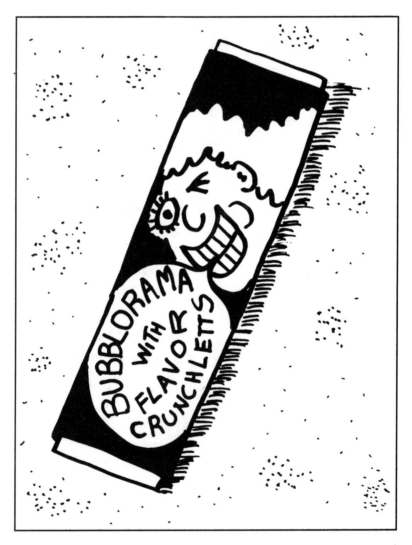

Pull The Old "Wanna Piece of (Phantom) Gum?" Trick

Ask a friend if they want some gum. If they say "Yes," give them the *phantom gum*. When they realize they've been fooled, you'll both *laugh till you cry!*

Doodle*Update*

Make A Hand Turkey

Trace your hand, and make it look like a turkey!
GOBBLE GOBBLE!

Sharpenmania

Sharpen a pencil until it's nothing but a point and an eraser. Why? Because it's an excellent way to improve coordination and strengthen finger muscles. *YEAH RIGHT!* Because it kills time and it's really *funny lookin'!*

Pick Some Eye Boogers

Pick the crispy nuggets from the corners of your eyes for hours of fun. *Collect em 'n' trade em!*

The Protruding Projectile Pencil

Place a pencil on your desk so that the pointed side is protruding out past the desk's edge*. Now with a smooth downward motion, whack the pencil where it's hanging over the edge, and *watch that baby go!*

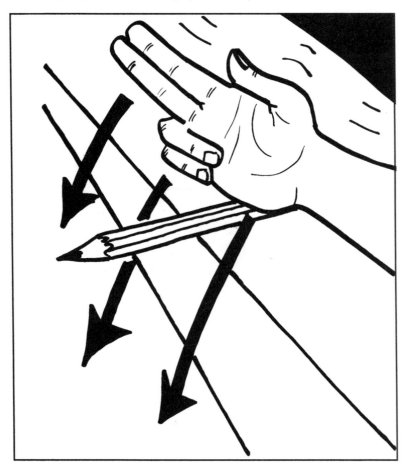

Make sure nobody is in the pencil's flight path.
Especially your boss or teacher.

Floss! Floss! Floss!

Why not take this opportunity to use a magazine page, or some other piece of paper to pick a little leftover lunch out of your teeth? *MMH MMH!* It tastes *even better* the second time around!

Decorate Your Pencil

Use a *pen* (felt tip for best results) and draw lines and stuff on your *pencil!* Imagine that! A pencil is used to write, and now *you're writing on IT! WHOA!* That really makes your head spin doesn't it?! *Man, I'm gettin' dizzy just thinkin' about it!*

Doodle*Update*

Patterns

Top artists from around the globe are paid big bucks to come up with patterns. That's right, patterns that you see every day on fabrics for clothing, furniture, and more! Make your own patterns. You won't see a red cent for any of 'em but it wastes time pretty good!

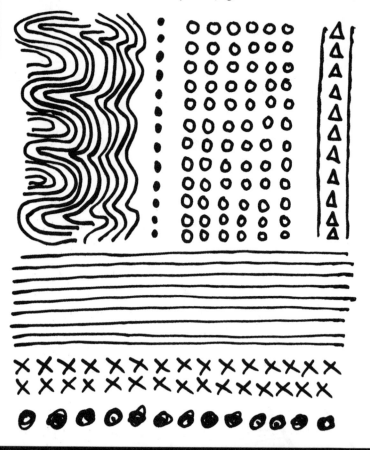

Check The Fax Machine

What's that you say? You're not expecting a fax. So what's your point? Read *other people's* faxes! That's right, *now you're getting the hang of this.*

Paint Stuff With Liquid Paper

CAREFUL though! It's easy to get carried away! Paint your pen, your notebook, paper clips, pads, your desk, fingernails, the bottom of your shoe, your lunch bag, your friend's lunch bag, your *friend, your whole desk, YOUR BOSS'S SHINY BALD HEAD...* *whoa!* See what I mean?!

Color In a Sticky Note Pad

Use a black magic marker to color in an entire sticky note pad. *DON'T FORGET THE SIDES!*

Make Money

Hold on now! Before you go running out and doing something productive to earn money, read on.

Place a coin under a piece of paper, and hold it in place. Then, scribble over the top of it with a pencil and, voila*! The coin's image appears on the page! Hey now! *Don't you try and spend those phonies, YOU COUNTERFEITER YOU!*

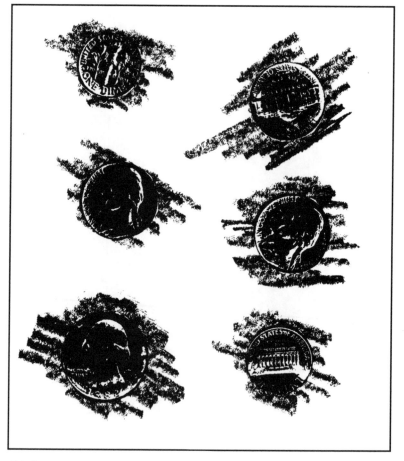

Voila: A French word meaning, "Well would you look at that!"

The Snooze Cruise

Put off going to that boring morning class by repeatedly pressing the snooze button on your alarm clock. Be sure to hit the button enough times so that it's impossible to get to class before it begins. Now, to avoid the embarrassment of walking in after class has started, *DON'T GO!*

Doodle*Update*

Cross Hatch Batch

Pen and ink artists have been using this technique for years to create shading in their works of art. Now you can use it to get through your miserable day! Here's how it works:

Step 1: Draw vertical lines, very close together, one next to the other.
Step 2: Crisscross horizontal lines on top of the vertical ones.
Step 3: Do the same with lines at 45 and 90 degrees.
Step 4: Repeat!

Each set of lines creates the illusion of darker shading. Use this technique in other doodlings!

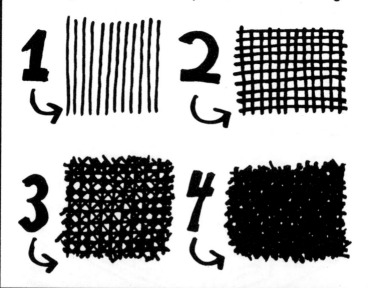

Strip a Pencil

Use a scissor blade to scrape all the paint off a pencil to achieve that *natural, woodsy, rustic look* that's so very popular these days.

Go To The Bathroom

Aaaah, the bathroom. The *procrastinator's amusement park.* There's *so much* to do in there! Look in the mirror, fix your hair, wash your hands, relieve yourself, or just sit on the toilet and ponder the hours away.

Asparagus

Whoops! Sorry! This is from 1001 WAYS TO *FLATULATE* not *PROCRASTINATE*.

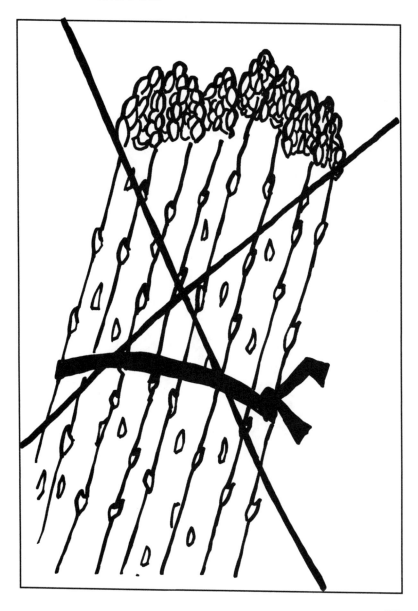

Bitch Bitch Bitch

Imagine A Yokefellow Being Pestered By a Swarm of Vespertilian

Not only can you amuse yourself by conjuring up this comical image, but in order to do so, *you have to use a dictionary! IT'S A DOUBLE TIME WASTER!*

Signal
The Allied Fleet

Make believe your stapler is a *Telegraph Machine* and pretend* to send messages by *Morse Code*.

*PRETEND is the operative word here. If you start to RECEIVE messages on your stapler, you may want to think about taking that vacation.

Create
Mr. Thumbtack Man

Make a face on your bulletin board using an assort-
ment of colored thumbtacks. Well *looky looky!* It's Mr.
Thumbtack Man! Hey Mr. Thumbtack Man, do you think
I should stop procrastinating, just for a minute, and get
something—*ANYTHING*—done?!

Doodle*Update*

Fingerprint Fun

Color in a heavily inked area on your note-book or desk, and press your thumb into it. Now imagine you're fingerprinting a danger-ous criminal! *Book 'em Danno!*

Examine Your Fingerprints

Look closely at your fingertips. See all those swirls and shapes formed by your fingerprints? Well, with a little imagination they can entertain you for hours as you look for familiar objects formed by the patterns. *Hey look! It's Elvis!* Hey King, do you think I should stop staring at my hands like a mental patient and get something done today?!

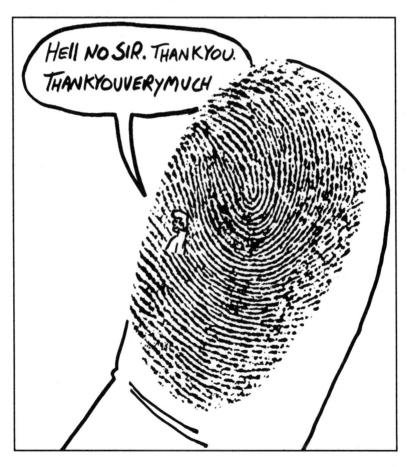

Imagine A Friend, Co-Worker, Or Stranger Naked

Wordumbers

Enter the number "7734" into an ordinary digital calculator. Now turn the calculator upside down and read the number as a word. *WOW, and a curse-word at that!* Now try numbers "55378008", and "07734". Make up your own words! *It's wordumberific!*

No ya big silly! It only works with a calculator.

Snack Time

Lick an envelope with a mint flavored glue strip for a cool refreshing midday snack.

Compile A List Of Ways To Procrastinate

Compile your own list of ways to procrastinate and *sell a million copies just like this book has!* O.K., maybe not a million, *100,000 copies!* O.K.... 5,000. 1000? Would you believe 500 copies? O.K.! My Mom read it! *And now you!*

The Elbow Coin Snatch

Step One: Place a quarter on your elbow thusly.
Step Two: With a quick downward motion bring your hand and forearm forward and try and snatch the coin before it falls. *Add a coin each time you make a successful catch!*

Go Buy A Refreshing Beverage

If you haven't lost all your change attempting the "Elbow Coin Snatch" then go to your nearest deli, grocer, or vending machine and purchase a tasty ice cold drink. With the plethora* of different fruit juice combinations and iced teas on the market today, just choosing one could take hours! So go on and get yourself that *Very Very Berry and Broccoli Iced Tea*. Or would you prefer the *Peach Guava 'N' Tuna Spritzer*?

Plethora: A word meaning: A-whole-helluvalotta

Doodle*Update*

Create An Animated Film

If you take your time with this one, you can *easily kill an entire day!* Take a thick notebook or pad and begin drawing whatever you wish (a stick figure, a face, a cute and highly marketable character suitable for licensing on lunch boxes and T-shirts). It's up to you. For our purposes we'll use this stick figure. Draw the figure. Then draw it again on the next page, only slightly different. Then again on the next page, but slightly different than the page before. Keep doing this on as many pages as you like. When you fan the pages, your figure *will APPEAR TO MOVE! Why, you're a regular WALT DISNEY!*

Make Up Excuses

Let's face it. With all the procrastinating you're doing you're bound to let a few things slip through the cracks. But don't be discouraged by your lack of responsibility, *use it to goof off some more!* Concoct elaborate webs of white lies to cover for all those things you were planning on doing before you started reading this book.

Playfully Annoy A Friend Or Co-Worker

Did you know you can waste away hours a day, and help others procrastinate, by simply annoying the people around you?! *Well it's true!*

Make Señor Hand Man

Use a pen to draw a little face on the side of your hand, then make him talk! Hey Señor Hand Man, I've got a whole truck load-a stuff I have to get done, but I'm gonna talk to you for a while instead. All right?

Create Fake Glue Fingerprints

If you're lucky enough to have some Elmer's Glue around you may never get *ANYTHING* done again! Squirt a little bit of glue out, and rub it on your fingertips coating them lightly. Allow the glue to air dry and… HOLY *GROUND UP HORSE BONES!* Fake fingerprints! Now peel the glue off and start all over. Put it on your whole hand! *It's fun! I don't know why, it just is!*

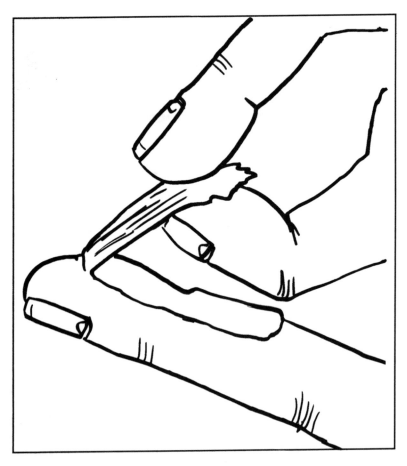

Get Some Water—
Let It Get Warm—
Get Some More

DoodleUpdate

Trace Stuff

Coins, pens, pencils, mugs, body parts, rulers,
paper clips, your keys, gum… WHATEVER!

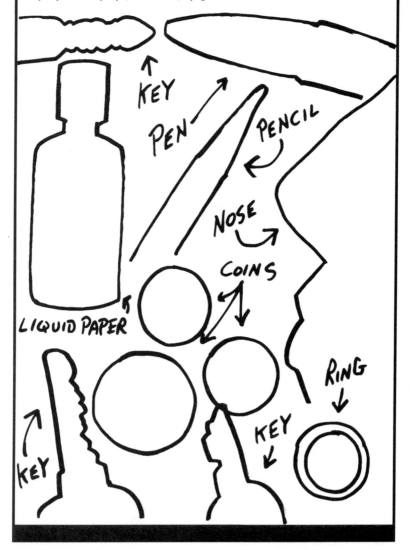

KEY

PEN

PENCIL

NOSE

COINS

LIQUID PAPER

RING

KEY

KEY

Pick Things Up
With Your Feet

Take your shoe off and pick up pencils and other
objects by curling your toes around them.

Reach Out
And Touch Yourself

HEY NOW! Let go of that THIS MINUTE! That's not what I mean! I mean call yourself and leave a message on your answering machine. Sheesh!

The Crazy Coin Balance

See how many coins you can stand on end. Nickels are easy. Dimes are *impossible!*

The Wacky Coin Spin

Once you've got those coins standing... SPIN *EM!*
WHEEEEEEEEEEEEEE! How many can you get spinning at
the same time?! *Five? Six? TEN?!*

Doodle*Update*

The Triple Utensil Stencil

Take three different writing devices, hold them together in one hand, and start scribbling! Try it with 4, 5, 6 different colors!

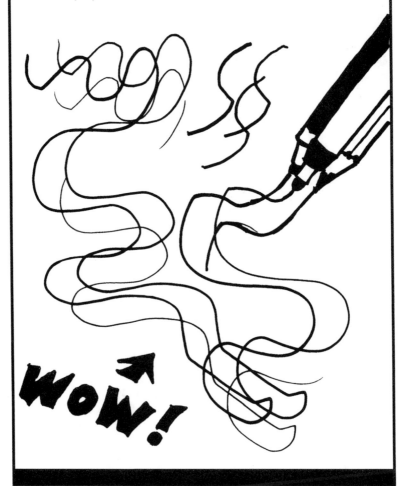

WOW!

Day Dream

Open up the front door and let your mind out to play!
Don't forget to tell it to be home by supper though.

Get Out A Calendar And Count The Days Till Your Birthday

Make a Spit Ball

Put a wad of paper into your mouth and work it into a slimy gooey mass of saliva laden pulp. Now throw it at something (or someone) *and watch it stick!* Why? *Why the heck not?!*

Doodle*Update*

Re-Touch Photos

Pick a photograph in a book, magazine or news-paper, and add your own elements.

For instance, look at the fun we can have by adding a few tattoos and some facial hair to this picture of a lovely bride!

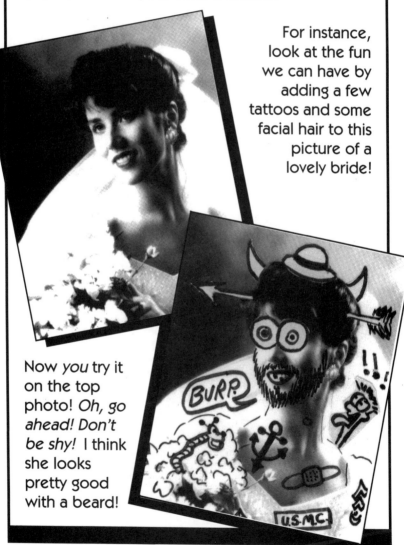

Now *you* try it on the top photo! *Oh, go ahead! Don't be shy!* I think she looks pretty good with a beard!

Wet-N-Wild

Ideal for students on Summer break! Fill up several balloons with the liquid of your choice (water, shaving cream, motor oil, mayonnaise, maple syrup). It all depends on the results you desire. Now go outside and heave 'em at your friends. This not only kills time while you fill the balloons and throw them, but afterwards too. *That's right!* Weeks after you ambush your pals you'll still be nervously looking over your shoulder waiting for their certain retaliation. Yep, there's never a dull moment while living in *CONSTANT FEAR OF REVENGE!*

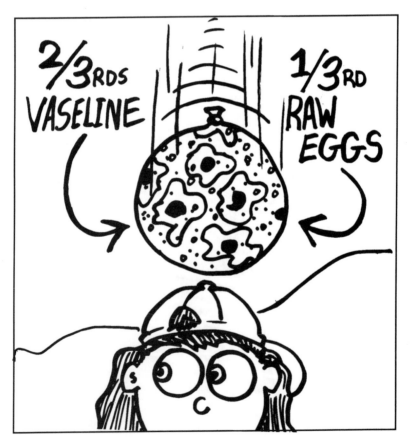

See How Many Times You Can Fold A Piece Of Paper

Take an ordinary piece of paper and keep folding it in half until you can't do it any more.

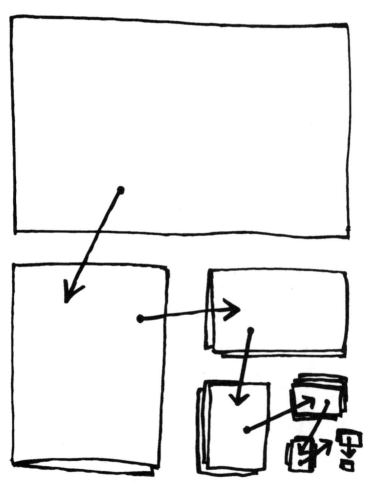

Juggle Juggle Juggle

Imagine yourself on Circus of the Stars, as you take ordinary objects and try to juggle them! *OOOPS!* *Excuse me Ms. Leggy Supermodel, but would you mind handing me that stapler. YOWZA!*

Count Your Teeth

Using the tip of your tongue, feel around inside your mouth and see if you can count how many teeth you have!*

*Counting someone else's teeth this way can be just as amusing. The only thing is you have to know them really, really, REALLY well. On the other hand, if you don't know 'em, you sure as hell will when you're done!

Make A Paper Snowflake

Remember back in kindergarten when you'd decorate your classroom with snowflakes made by cutting shapes into folded pieces of paper? Well now you can use those childhood lessons to goof off as an adult. *Ah, the memories. Makes ya just want to eat some paste.*

Doodle_Update_

The Never-Ending Stupendous Spiral Of Outrageous Fun

Much like *The Super Colossal Never-Ending Star Of Eternal Bliss,* this doodle can go on forever! Just pick a point and start spiraling outward! *Careful now! Don't get yourself dizzy!*

Pick An Orifice
And Pick Away

The human body has countless openings (ears, nose, scabs, etc.). Choose your favorite and pick! pick! pick! *Now, don't be shy!* You're not alone. Not everybody picks everything, but we all pick somethin'!

Make A Brontosaurus With Your Hand

Whoa! Look at that! A miniature dinosaur just by holding your hand thusly. Make another one with your other hand and *have 'em fight! GRRRR!*

Look Yourself Up In The Phone Book

See how many other people in town have your name. Do you think they're related? Call 'em up and ask!

Build Eraser Furniture

Using a large eraser and some thumb tacks you can craft your own mini furniture. Like this attractive dining room table, for example.

Make Gum Pottery

Take a well-chewed piece of gum and mold it into a miniature masterpiece. Allow the gum to dry for a few days and look what an attractive accessory this mini vase makes for your eraser table! Add some flowers fashioned from toothpicks and bits of paper and...
LOOK *OUT BETTER HOMES AND GARDENS!*

Eavesdrop

Listen to other peoples conversations. Take notes. Use the information against them later if you can!

Scribble

That's right! Plain and simple. Just scribble! It's fun and it's a great way to get rid of the frustration you feel because your procrastinating has prevented you from doing all those things you were supposed to do.

Do Something Productive

AAH HA HA HA HA HA HA HA HA HA HA HA HA HA!!!
JUST KIDDING!

Construct Paper Airplanes

Using ordinary pieces of paper, create your own mini air force.

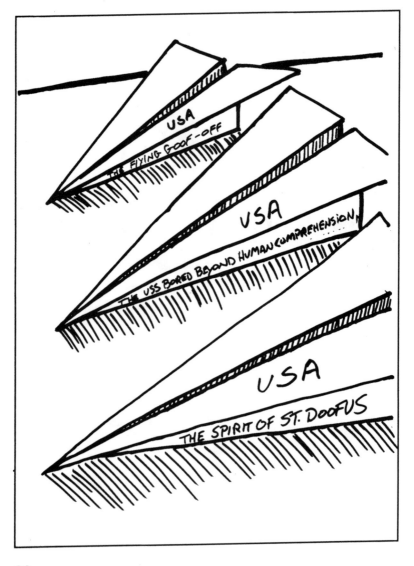

Fly Your Paper Airplanes

Try and fly those little planes. When you find that they don't fly very well, see page 16 (Origami Snowballs).

Craft Fine HomeMade Jewelry

Use paper clips and rubber bands to make attractive personal accessories. Necklaces. Bracelets. *Even Earrings!*

The Space Pencil

Trace your pencil, then turn it into a *rocket ship!* Place it on a launch pad, or *soaring through the Milky Way!*

Make A Spectacle Of Yourself

Take a quarter (a half dollar if you have one) and stick it in your eye like it's a spectacle. Pretend you're F.D.R.! Or, *better yet,* Colonel Klink from that wacky Nazi sit-com: *Hogan's Heros!* Don't let your boss catch you or you'll get sent to the *Russian front!*

Create Coin People

Using different combinations of coins, create your own pocket change pals. *Well, look here! It's Mr. 30 Cents!* Hey, Mr. 30 Cents, do you think I should stop procrastinating and try to get something done?

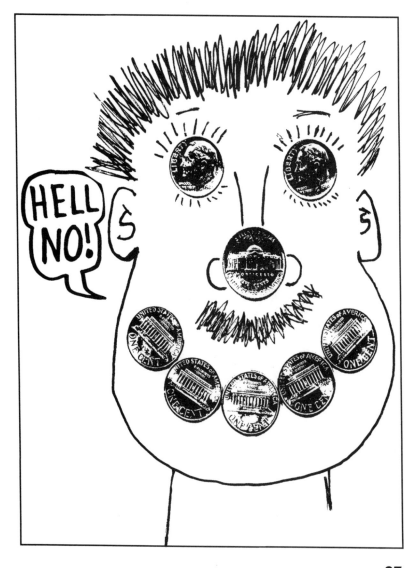

Look Up Dirty Words In The Dictionary

Ever wonder if some of your favorite off-color slang has made it into the dictionary? Well don't just sit there! Get out that @#%!*@# Webster's and *look the @#%!*@# thing up!*

Key Inventory

Take out your key chain and see if you can mentally identify which keys go to which locks*. Find that one key that you haven't used in years, but are afraid to throw out in case you need it. What the hell does that thing open anyway?

*If you're a janitor this can be extremely challenging and, most of all, time consuming.

Fun With Time

Call for the exact time, and set your watch.

Fun With Breathing And Time

Use your watch to time just how long you can hold your breath. Don't forget to start breathing again or... well... you'll die. And, while dying is an excellent time waster, it's reportedly no fun.

Practice Your Signature

Do you envy those people who have really cool signatures? Don't you wish you had one? Well you can! Simply practice signing your name any way you want to, over and over and over and over. *Whoa! This one almost borders on pro-ductive! Gotta watch that.*

JOHN HANCOCK   *John Hancock*

Johng Boy Hancock   **JOHN HANCOCK**

John Hancock II   *J.H.*

J. HANCOCKAROO

John Alowishus SHEMP HANCOCK

JOHN HANCOCK   *FABIO*

Play Some Skins

Take a couple pencils or pens and play drums on the objects around you.

Pencil Mustache

See if you can hold a pencil, or any other object between your upper lip and nose. Some people can do it, others can't. If you're one of the lucky ones, be thankful for your special gift.

Left Is Write

If you're right-handed, try to write your name with your left hand. If you're left-handed, try it with your right hand. If you're ambidextrous... never mind.

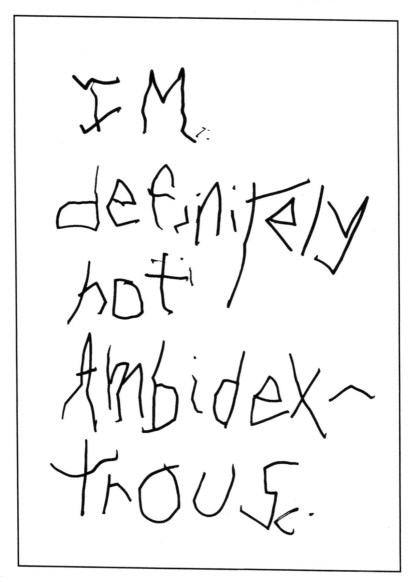

Fun With Forgery

Practice someone's signature until you've got it *just right*. If you're under 18, try it with your parent's signatures. It can come in handy… *reeeeeal handy!*

REPORT CARD

ENGLISH............................D
SCIENCE........................F-
ALGEBRA....................F
SOCIAL STUDIES........D-
MUSIC..............................F
ART....................................A

COMMENTS: *often procrastinates!*

X *Tony's Mom*

PARENT'S SIGNATURE

Make Rubber Cement Boogers

Spread a thin layer of rubber cement on a piece of paper and allow it to dry. Now rub your finger over the area until the cement begins to turn into, *of all things, little boogers!*

Pull The Old "You've Got A (Rubber Cement) Booger On You" Trick

Approach a friend or co-worker* and quickly rub a rubber cement booger on their hand or arm. Then say, *"EEEW! You've got a booger on you!"* Then pause and coyly say, "A *rubber cement* booger, that is!" If you don't say that last part they'll think you're kinda gross—not to mention, unsanitary.

*Avoid doing this to someone you've only known for a short time.

Cable

OK so you're probably wondering where the other several hundred or so ways to procrastinate are, aren't you? You're probably thinkin: "Hey pal! This book is called *1001 Ways To Procrastinate*. Where's the rest?!" Yeah, ya know I've really been meaning to get around to writing those...

I wonder what's on TV...

About The Author

The author, hard at work in his Washington DC studio.

Tony Rubino was born just outside of Tempe, Arizona in 1897, and raised by Comanche Indians. He was a mighty warrior, killing his first man at the age of 12. Well... OK, I'm exaggerating a little bit. He was born in New Jersey in 1966 and raised by Italians. And he didn't kill that guy till he was 15—and it wasn't a guy, it was a spider... OK, the spider got away.

When he's not procrastinating, Tony contributes to various publications, including *National Lampoon*, *MAD Magazine* and *Cracked Magazine*. He also writes and draws his nationally syndicated cartoons, *Pregnant Pause* and *Wild Kingdom, Featuring Mr. College*. These cartoons are distributed to over 400 newspapers every week. In addition, his cartoons and designs appear on dozens of greeting cards, posters, T-shirts, mugs, and other assorted impulse items. Look for them in stores and catalogs everywhere.

TITLES BY CCC PUBLICATIONS

NEW PARTY BOOKS (Available: May 1994)

Retail $4.99

THINGS YOU CAN DO WITH A USELESS MAN

FLYING FUNNIES

MARITAL BLISS & OTHER OXYMORONS

THE VERY VERY SEXY DOT-TO-DOT BOOK

BASTARD'S GUIDE TO BUSINESS SURVIVAL

THE DEFINITIVE FART BOOK

THE TOTAL WIMP'S GUIDE TO SEX

THE CAT OWNER'S SHAPE-UP MANUAL

LIFE'S MOST EMBARRASSING MOMENTS

PMS CRAZED: TOUCH ME & I'LL KILL YOU!

RETIRED: LET THE GAMES BEGIN

MALE BASHING: WOMEN'S FAVORITE PASTIME

THE OFFICE FROM HELL

FOOD & SEX

BUT OSSIFER, IT'S NOT MY FAULT

YOU KNOW YOU'RE AN OLD FART WHEN...

HOW TO REALLY PARTY!!!

HOW TO SURVIVE A JEWISH MOTHER – **Oct.**

1994 NEW TRADE PAPERBACKS – Retail $4.95

SHARING THE ROAD WITH IDIOTS

GREATEST ANSWERING MACHINE MESSAGES

1001 WAYS TO PROCRASTINATE – **May**

FITNESS FANATICS – **Jun.**

THE WORLD'S GREATEST PUT-DOWN LINES – **Jun.**

HORMONES FROM HELL II – **May**

YOUNGER MEN ARE BETTER THAN RETIN-A – **Jul.**

RED HOT MONOGAMY – **($6.95) Jul.**

ROSS PEROT: DON'T QUOTE ME – **Sep.**

BEST SELLING TRADE PAPERBACKS – Retail $4.95
HORMONES FROM HELL **($5.95)**
KILLER BRAS & OTHER HAZARDS OF THE 50'S
BETTER TO BE OVER THE HILL THAN UNDER IT
HUSBANDS FROM HELL
HOW TO ENTERTAIN PEOPLE YOU HATE
THE UGLY TRUTH ABOUT MEN
WHAT DO WE DO NOW??
TALK YOUR WAY OUT OF A TRAFFIC TICKET
THE BOTTOM HALF

BEST SELLING TRADE PAPERBACKS – Retail $3.95
NO HANG-UPS
NO HANG-UPS II
NO HANG-UPS III
GETTING EVEN WITH THE ANSWERING MACHINE
NEVER A DULL CARD
WORK SUCKS!
THE PEOPLE WATCHER'S FIELD GUIDE
THE UNOFFICIAL WOMEN'S DIVORCE GUIDE
YOUR GUIDE TO CORPORATE SURVIVAL
THE ABSOLUTE LAST CHANCE DIET BOOK
FOR MEN ONLY (How To Survive Marriage)
SUPERIOR PERSON'S GUIDE TO IRRITATIONS
GIFTING RIGHT
HOW TO GET EVEN WITH YOUR EXes
HOW TO SUCCEED IN SINGLES BARS
OUTRAGEOUS BUMPER-SNICKERS **($2.95)**

ACCESSORIES
THE GUILT BAG **($4.95)**
THE "MAGIC BOOKMARK" BOOK COVER **($2.95)**

NO HANG-UPS – CASSETTES – Retail $4.98
Vol. I: GENERAL MESSAGES
Vol. II: BUSINESS MESSAGES
Vol. III: 'R' RATED MESSAGES
Vol. IV: SOUND EFFECTS ONLY
Vol. V: CELEBRI-TEASE